MILITARY INTELLIGENCE TECHNOLOGY OF THE FUTURE

Dominic J. Caraccilo

The Rosen Publishing Group, Inc., New York

For Jenna, Jacob, and Robert, my great kids

Published in 2006 by The Rosen Publishing Group, Inc.
29 East 21st Street, New York, NY 10010

Library of Congress Cataloging-in-Publication Data

Caraccilo, Dominic J. (Dominic Joseph), 1962–
Military intelligence technology of the future / Dominic J. Caraccilo.—1st ed.
    p. cm.—(The library of future weaponry)
Includes bibliographical references and index.
ISBN 1-4042-0528-4 (library binding)
1. Military intelligence—Juvenile literature. I. Title. II. Series.
UB250.C36 2006
355.3'432—dc22

              2005019303

Manufactured in the United States of America

On the cover: A test model of the U.S. Army's future unmanned aerial vehicle
known as the Warrior. The Warrior will be used to spy on enemy troops and
territory.

CONTENTS

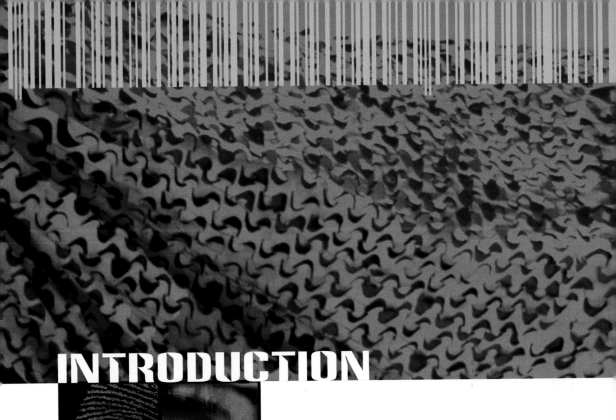

INTRODUCTION

There are numerous challenges to peace and security in the twenty-first century. Some of these challenges are new and some of them have been around for centuries. One of the greatest challenges today is how to combat a rise in international terrorism. Military authorities are also concerned about problems such as the spread of weapons of mass destruction and the international drug trade. These developments have brought about a shift in how the military goes about gathering information about potential enemies. This gathering of information is called military intelligence.

Military intelligence personnel use many different methods and strategies to get the job done. These include surveillance, reconnaissance, threat analysis, electronic warfare, and various combat communications systems. These methods, and the technology behind them, will be the focus of this book.

Much has been done by the military to develop systems, train personnel, and define the role of military intelligence in the future. An important part of the future military force will be an increasing reliance on computer technology. This technology will allow soldiers to receive and exchange information faster than ever before. The end result will be an army better able to defeat the enemy.

SEEING THE BATTLESPACE

Military intelligence is concerned with learning about the enemy, both before and during battle. In military conflicts, it is extremely important to be able to identify friend from foe and to have a clear understanding of where fellow troops are located, in addition to the location of the enemy. Military commanders strive to have a complete understanding of these factors, which is known as situational awareness.

The location of a battle, including the land, sea, and air above, is known as the battlefield or the battlespace. Seeing the battlespace in its entirety is a crucial part of military intelligence.

Today's technology allows commanders, military intelligence personnel, and soldiers in the midst of battle to view the battlespace on a computer screen. Enemy locations, friendly troop locations, weather information, and terrain

A U.S. marine examines a Dragon Eye unmanned aerial vehicle (UAV). Dragon Eye is a remotely controlled aircraft with mounted cameras used to spy on enemy troops and territory. UAVs like Dragon Eye play a critical role in military intelligence and will continue to do so in the future.

characteristics can all be displayed. Those involved in the fighting can keep track of the battle and devise strategies based on their understanding of the entire battlespace.

THE ROLE OF THE COMMANDER

The commander drives intelligence. He or she is responsible for making clear what needs to be known about the enemy. The commander puts together a plan used by intelligence personnel to get key information at the right time. This allows the commander to make the decisions necessary to win battles. To achieve this goal, the commander uses a wide array of technologies that help him or her gain an understanding of where the enemy is and what the enemy's capabilities are.

FRIEND OR FOE?

A good example of how technology will be used to detect friend from foe is the Individual Combat Identification System (ICIDS). Currently in development, this system will help in minimizing deaths due to friendly fire, which is when a soldier accidentally kills another soldier in the same force.

The system consists of two units: the interrogator and the transponder. The interrogator is a device that is mounted on a soldier's weapon. It creates a beam of infrared energy that is recognized by a transponder, which is a helmet-mounted receiver. A soldier carrying an interrogator can use it to identify friendly troops by aiming it at an unidentified soldier. If the target is wearing a transponder, a message will be sent back to the interrogator in the form of a simple code that identifies the target as a friend.

In the future, ICIDS will be part of the Land Warrior system. Land Warrior is a high-tech, futuristic combination of weaponry and equipment for the infantry soldier.

THE ENEMY TODAY

Enemy forces in the world today use creative tactics and do not stick to traditional battle plans. This is because the adversaries of today have realized that the U.S. military is difficult to defeat on open terrain in which the U.S. can concentrate its weapons and forces.

However, what the enemies of the United States have learned from experience is that the will of the American public and its allies can be affected. Therefore, the enemy focuses on finding a way to break the spirit of its adversary. Sometimes, the enemy will go after nonmilitary targets, so there is little risk of having to battle in a conventional way. The 9/11 attacks are an example of this strategy. Trying to understand the strategy and mind-set of the enemy is the first step in how military intelligence technology of the future will attempt to defeat this creative and elusive enemy.

BATTLE COMMAND

Effective battle command focuses on seeing the battlefield as clearly as possible. Commanders want to closely track forces,

The U.S. military expects most future warfare to take place in urban set-tings. To prepare for tomorrow's urban battles, virtual reality training systems have been developed. In this photo, a soldier uses binoculars to identify targets in a computer-generated city. Virtual soldiers are projected on the wall to the left of the trainee.

both enemy and friendly. They also want to know about the terrain, weather, or anything else that might affect the battle. Further, they are looking for a way to take in all of this information as quickly and accurately as possible. Commanders will use all this information to predict and anticipate enemy actions. With the technology on hand today, commanders have the ability to "see" the battlefield better than ever before.

The intelligence part of battle command has two key parts. The first is the need for quick access to information about the enemy. The military doesn't want any delay between when something happens and when a command post learns about it. If there is too much of a delay, then the intelligence may not be meaningful anymore. For example, a spy plane might report that an enemy force is approaching. But if the intelligence doesn't reach the commander in time, it may be too late to prevent an attack.

The military is also concerned about being able to predict what the enemy may do. This requires a combination of smart human experts and sophisticated computer systems. Together, these two elements gather data and analyze it in an attempt to predict enemy formations, strength, and locations.

THE GOAL OF TECHNOLOGY

The ultimate goal in military intelligence is to use technology to better understand the enemy. The main technology to meet this goal is intelligence, surveillance, and reconnaissance (ISR) technology, which we will look at in greater detail in the next

Soldiers of the 101st Airborne Division are hard at work at a battle command center in Iraq. Command centers such as this one are vital to military operations. One of the most important functions of the command center is to process military intelligence and pass it on to commanders as quickly as possible.

chapter. Also important is the sharing of information among intelligence groups at all levels and throughout all the services in the military (army, air force, marines, and navy). The military intelligence soldier combines these technologies in order to complete his or her mission.

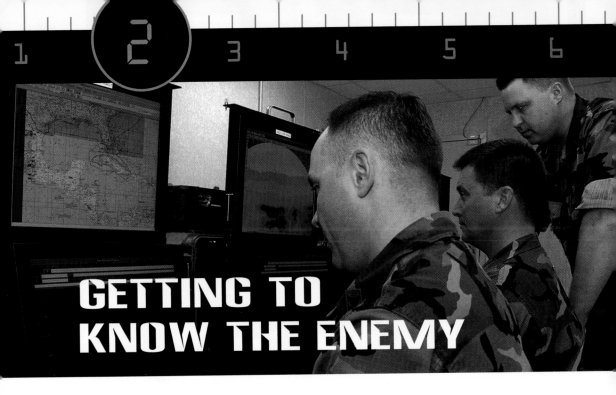

GETTING TO KNOW THE ENEMY

Intelligence, surveillance, and reconnaissance, or what is commonly referred to as ISR, is a vital part of all military operations. ISR is how the military learns about the enemy.

Intelligence is defined as information and knowledge about an enemy obtained through observation, investigation, and analysis. The two main methods used to gather intelligence are reconnaissance and surveillance. Reconnaissance is the exploration and survey of an enemy area. It usually occurs shortly before a military attack. Surveillance involves the observation of an area by visual, electronic, or photographic equipment. In the military, surveillance and reconnaissance may be accomplished by aircraft or satellites in the sky, soldiers on the ground, ships at sea, or other means.

Pictured above is the Mobile Integrated Geospatial Intelligence System (MIGS). The system consists of three high-tech computers and a satellite dish. It is used to gather intelligence from many different sources and make it available to soldiers. This intelligence might include pictures of enemy camps, weather forecasts, or maps of the battlefield.

The goal of ISR operations is to provide commanders with the information they need to make quick and effective decisions. ISR operations are the eyes and ears of the military.

ISR becomes more useful to the operator if the data acquired from ISR systems can be translated to other users over combat communications systems. These systems include state-of-the-art radio systems, the Internet, and satellite-based computer systems.

Acquiring data on the enemy is important. Doing it fast is critical. However, data and information are not the same thing. For example, the rate of movement of an enemy force is data. It is analyzed to provide the commander with useful information. In this example, the data might be analyzed to predict the time of an attack and where it will take place. This information will help the commander take action. Many technological systems exist today to accomplish these tasks.

STORING DATA

Military intelligence requires accurate computer databases. These databases store and sort the vast amount of data collected on the enemy. Data within a database might include the names of enemy leaders, battlefield targets, enemy formations, enemy strength, types of uniforms, and many other types of data. This data is analyzed to produce graphics and text that are used to come up with battle and security plans. The goal for the future is to make these technologies faster and more reliable.

In the future, it will also be important for military intelligence to be able to share data with units up and down the chain of command. (For example, from a squad to a platoon to a company to a battalion. Each of these units is larger than the one that precedes it. A squad has about nine soldiers, while a battalion consists of 300 to 1,000 soldiers.) Today, many units use different types of equipment. New technology is required to link all these systems and make them more useful.

ISR IN THE ARMY

The United States is currently transforming its ISR technology. New ideas, experiments, and organizational changes are about to change the way the army operates. Increasing the ability to see and understand the battlespace is one of the most important areas of research. Three different technologies are central to the army of the future. These are the Future Combat Systems, unmanned aerial vehicles, and the Army Battle Command System.

THE FUTURE OF MILITARY SYSTEMS

The Future Combat Systems (FCS) is a massive project of the U.S. Army. It will use advanced communications and technologies to link the soldier with different kinds of data-gathering sensors.

The FCS soldier will wear a helmet with an attached video display to allow the soldier to view mission data. Advanced communications software called the

On the network, the strong become stronger.

FCS

THE US ARMY'S FUTURE COMBAT SYSTEMS. It's the foundation of the Future Force. By creating fully-networked systems that are interoperable with joint and allied forces, FCS-equipped Units of Action will be stronger, faster, more agile and more effective. The best-of-industry FCS One Team is making this vision a reality, delivering on all program requirements to give the warfighter unrivaled strength in any battlespace.

WWW.ARMY.MIL/FCS

The U.S. Army has released this poster to advertise the Future Combat Systems. A major goal of the FCS is to increase the speed at which the army can respond to threats all over the world. Improved military intelligence will be key to attaining this goal.

Warfighter Information Network-Tactical (WIN-T) will be the backbone of the FCS. WIN-T provides what is known as C4ISR support. C4ISR stands for command, control, communications, computers, intelligence, surveillance, and reconnaissance.

It is expected that the first FCS will be available in 2014. Included in the five technologies that will be produced for the FCS are unattended ground sensors, two classes of unmanned aerial vehicles (UAVs), and armed robotic vehicles. FCS units will enable the army to see first, understand first, act first, and win battles decisively.

This future force will be lighter and more mobile. The army hopes to be able to put a combat-ready brigade anywhere in the world within 96 hours, a full division in 120 hours, and five divisions on the ground within 30 days.

BIG BROTHER IS WATCHING

Unmanned aerial vehicles are quickly becoming the vehicles of choice for intelligence, surveillance, and reconnaissance. UAVs are airplanes of various sizes that are remotely controlled. The information they gather as they fly over enemy territory can be transmitted instantaneously to the operator and troops on the ground. UAVs provide a safer way for information collection since a pilot is not lost if the aircraft is shot down or crashes.

Besides being safer to use, UAVs provide a number of benefits for collecting ISR data. They can provide what is called persistent surveillance, which is the ability to circle over the

A Predator UAV taxis down the runway in Iraq on March 31, 2005. The soldier with the cord around his neck is the external pilot. His job is to guide the UAV during takeoff and landing. There are also internal pilots, located at a ground station, who control the UAV while it is in flight.

same area for a long period of time. Their persistence makes it difficult for the enemy to hide its activities since the UAV will always be overhead. By contrast, many satellites or manned airplanes can view areas only periodically, which makes it easier for the enemy to hide or disguise what it is doing.

UAVs allow a commander to get a better picture of what is going on in the battlespace. The persistent coverage of UAVs provides the commander with very accurate data on enemy locations and strength. This data can be used to guide weapons against the enemy. UAVs also give warfighters a sense of what is happening on the battlefield at all times.

TYPES OF UAVs

The Predator is a type of UAV that operates at 15,000 to 25,000 feet (4,572 to 7,620 meters). It can stay airborne for up to forty hours. It normally carries special cameras and surveillance equipment that allow it to see in all weather conditions.

The Global Hawk is the largest UAV in existence. The Global Hawk flies at altitudes of up to 65,000 feet (19,812 m). That is nearly twice as high as commercial airliners can fly. The Global Hawk can stay in the air for twenty-four hours. During this time, it can survey an area as large as the state of Illinois.

Gridlock is a future system to help locate enemy targets. The system can pinpoint the target to within ten meters of its actual location. It can also help shorten what is called the kill chain. This is the process that starts with the detection of an enemy target, then leads to the firing of a weapon, and ends with the destruction of the target.

The smallest of all UAVs today is called the Raven. The Raven's wingspan is 4.5 feet (1.4 m). Because of its light weight (3.8 pounds, or 1.7 kilograms), it can be hand-launched. The Raven can fly at altitudes up to 1,000 feet (305 m). Once in the air, it can travel 6 to 9 miles (10 to 15 km) while surveying enemy locations and troop strength. It is something a commander can use to gain a better understanding of the battlespace. For instance, if a commander is approaching a hilltop and wants to know what is happening on the other side, he can launch his Raven. The Raven will survey the area and send back video

A U.S. army soldier launches a Raven UAV in Samarra, Iraq, during Operation Iraqi Freedom. The Raven can be set up and launched in under ten minutes. After its mission, it is disassembled and stored in three small carrying cases. Each Raven costs about $35,000, which is a bargain for a UAV.

images to the commander. Then the commander can decide if it is safe to cross over the hilltop.

ARMY BATTLE COMMAND SYSTEM

Many different communications systems have been combined to create the Army Battle Command System (ABCS). The need for this system was recognized more than a decade ago. Back then, communications systems relied on radio transmissions. However, military operation in the 1990s proved that radio transmission would not be sufficient and that the army also needed to transmit video and sound recordings from the battlefield.

The success of military operations in the future will depend on the rapid exchange of all types of information. Similar to the world of the Internet, the army will operate in a hyperlinked digital world. The ABCS is the heart of this new digital world. It consists of a complex set of systems that will enable leaders to know the precise positions of enemy and friendly forces. The following is a list of some of the systems and their roles.

AFATDS Advanced Field Artillery Tactical Data System. Helps artillery units locate and fire upon the enemy.

AMDWS Air and Missile Defense Workstation. Provides awareness of the air defense battlespace.

ASAS All Source Analysis System. Maintains information about the enemy in a computer database.

BCS3 Battle Command and Sustainment Support System. Provides a variety of information to commanders in the form of maps.

CTIS Combat Terrain Information Systems. Provides commanders with analysis of the terrain of a battlefield.

TAIS Tactical Airspace Integration System. Coordinates air traffic in the battlespace.

GCCS Global Command and Control System. Provides command and control at the highest levels of the army. It also communicates with the command and control systems of the other services.

IMETS Integrated Meteorological System. Provides commanders with information about the weather and how it may affect the battle.

THE NEED FOR A VERSATILE SOLDIER

Overall, the army and the other services are aiming to make their many different computer and communications systems more compatible. Today, each service, and many units within the same service, use their own systems. Often these systems use different parts and technologies and cannot communicate with each other. A major goal of the future is to redesign the systems so that they can work together.

To reach these goals, the military must also train and prepare its soldiers. They are, after all, the ones who will be responsible for operating this sophisticated new equipment and weaponry. While there continues to be a need for people with specific skills, the number of these specialists required will decrease. The result is a need for a skilled soldier capable of handling a wide variety of tasks. These soldiers of the future must be able to gather and present information to the commander for a complete understanding of the battlespace.

THE DIGITAL BATTLEFIELD

The technologies designed to improve ISR are part of the military's plan to digitize the entire battlefield. Some of the ideas under consideration to support this effort include developing better sensors, improving ISR integration and processing speed, and reducing what is known as a forward footprint.

BETTER SENSORS

Sensors are a critical part of the ISR mission. A sensor is a device that detects something either visually or by some other signal (light or sound, for example). Developing sensors that can be used by many different types of equipment is an important goal of the military. Today, many sensors work only with a specific system. Sensors in the future will be designed so that the information they receive can be

The Dragon Runner uses video, audio, and motion sensors to collect information about the enemy. The 9-pound (4.1 kg) robot is battery powered and can be carried in a backpack. It is currently being tested by marines in Iraq in limited numbers. If it performs well, the military will likely add more of these robot warriors to the force.

passed on to a unit regardless of the exact types of computer technology they use.

Efforts are being made to develop a family of sensors that extend from the ground to air to space. On the ground, the sensors will consist of microsensors, robots, and vehicles. In the air, the sensors will be found on manned and unmanned aircraft. In space, the sensors will be attached to satellites.

ISR INTEGRATION

Like with sensors, different intelligence systems need to be able to effectively communicate with each other. Also, data received from the sensors and human sources, such as an intelligence agent or the police, needs to be received by all the different systems. This data may be in the form of radio, video, digital messages, or text. And the data must reach all levels of the military, including the headquarters as well as the soldiers in combat situations.

Once data is gathered, it must be altered in a way that is useful to the commander and the soldier. This task is known as data processing. Therefore, making computer data processors smaller, faster, and more efficient is a goal of future ISR systems. When information can be collected and passed on very quickly, more information can be shared by more users in a shorter period of time.

The military has a phrase it uses for the ideal time it should take for information to get passed on. It's called real-time processing, which means the information is received by whoever needs it at the same time it is received by the sensor. The military seeks real-time or near real-time processing with all its technologies.

REDUCED FORWARD FOOTPRINT

The military is also developing systems that will reduce the forward footprint. "Forward footprint" is a term used to describe the location of military intelligence troops and technology on the battlefield. Ideally, they should be as far away from the enemy as possible. This keeps the troops, surveillance system, UAV, or whatever sensor device is being used out of harm's way. It also helps ensure that the enemy will not know it is being spied on.

ISR SYSTEM OF SYSTEMS

The success of combat operations depends to a large extent on the ability of the ISR system of systems (SoS). In an SoS, the individual parts can be very different but work together to collect information from many sources. A system of systems is like an orchestra in which all the instruments work together to create music. In an SoS, different sensors, UAVs, and human agents work together to create a clear picture of the enemy.

SENSING THE BATTLEFIELD

An example of a sensor used in the military today is the Remote Battlefield Sensor System (REMBASS). This system detects and tracks the movement of enemy personnel and vehicles. It works in all weather and during both the day and night. Future systems will be half the size of current versions of the system.

REMBASS consists of passive sensors. These are sensors that detect the enemy as it passes as opposed to those that seek out the enemy. Once in place, REMBASS can be left unattended for up to thirty days. When a target comes into range, the sensors can detect sound, heat, or magnetic fields produced by the target. The sensors then identify what kind of target it is (a person or a vehicle, for example). This information is translated into short digital messages and sent to a monitoring device. The monitoring device decodes the information and displays it for the user.

The information collected by the ISR systems is said to be "fused," which means to be mixed together. The information might concern the enemy, weather, or terrain in a specified geographic area.

There are many different ISR systems. They range from complex satellite-based video technology to information received from an individual soldier. Most ISR systems work together with computer databases accessible by forces in the air, on the sea, and on the ground. As this information is pulled from ISR systems in the field, it forms a picture of the battlespace. Through the digital ABCS systems, the picture of the battlespace is displayed on a computer. This picture is shared so that everyone involved in the war effort has access to the same information.

TESTING THE TECHNOLOGY

As future systems are added, it will be important to measure how well they are working. Any system that is not behaving as expected might have a negative effect on the overall military intelligence effort. Therefore, new systems will be evaluated on a regular basis to ensure they are acting as planned.

Another challenge concerns understanding and keeping track of all the various types of data available. ISR systems evaluate environmental conditions such as terrain and weather. They keep track of the movements of enemy forces while also keeping track of friendly forces. At the same time, the systems must be able to identify civilians in order to

Two employees of the Boeing Corporation chat at a convention hosted by the U.S. Air Force. Military intelligence technology is a competitive business in which billions of dollars are at stake. A convention such as this allows defense manufacturers such as Boeing and the U.S. military to discuss and plan future projects.

minimize collateral damage. These are just a few examples of the many different types of data that need to be tracked in a battle.

KEYS TO SUCCESS

One of the keys to success in military intelligence is being able to provide information to multiple networks. Some of these networks may have special restrictions while others will not. For example, information might be relayed to Department of Defense (DOD) networks that reach all DOD employees. Or information may be relayed to intelligence agency networks that require secret clearances. Or information may be sent to army networks that will be accessible only to higher-ups in the U.S. Army. In other words, data and information must be shared but not shared equally.

FUTURE PROJECTS

A number of technologies are being developed to help tie together all the military's information networks. Let's take a look at some of these current and future projects.

Global Information Grid

The Global Information Grid (GIG) is the military's version of the Internet. In the past, the sharing of intelligence was hindered by the slow movement of information through the military's computer networks. There has been a great effort to improve these networks to allow more information to flow faster.

Joint Tactical Radio System

This consists of radio technology that can be programmed like computers. It will help ensure that different military commands are able to communicate with each other.

Wideband Satellite Communications

This technology can be used by both civilian and military users. "Wideband" refers to a wide bandwidth, meaning that large amounts of information can pass from source to receiver very quickly. The Defense Department has been experimenting with wideband commercial satellite communications for several years. Today, this technology can be seen in satellite TV networks. The technology is also being developed for military use. The goal is to provide satellite feeds so that commanders can communicate with a command post using video as they move about the battlefield.

Net-Centric Enterprise Services

This provides services to support the broad range of applications and data used in the military intelligence computer networks.

Information Assurance

This helps ensure that the network is reliable and safe from attack by hackers or the enemy.

Horizontal Fusion

These are computer applications to help analysts and warfighters make sense of complex data that passes over the network.

THE COMMON GROUND STATION

The network is an extremely important part of ISR operations in the future. Within the network, information is shared by many different users. These users include the military and federal agencies such as the FBI and CIA.

The Common Ground Station (CGS) is the control center of the U.S. Army's military intelligence network. The CGS receives and processes data from multiple real-time sensors and systems.

The Common Ground Station (CGS) is a mobile communications center. The U.S. Army has more than 100 of these systems in operation. The computer hardware and software of the CGS has been designed so that it can be easily upgraded. This means that the CGS will continue to be an important part of military intelligence for many more years.

These include unmanned aerial vehicles, imagery intelligence (IMINT), signal intelligence (SIGINT), electronic intelligence (ELINT), and other sources.

The CGS is a mobile system that supports a wide range of global missions. These missions include battlefield management, crisis management, peacekeeping operations, and missions to combat the international drug trade. The CGS can operate in many different climates and weather conditions. It allows commanders to see situations more clearly than ever before and make firm and informed decisions.

CURRENT AIR AND GROUND CAPABILITIES

We've discussed many of the ways the military will improve its ISR systems in this chapter. Two exciting technologies already in use include the Quick Fix and the Prophet.

EH-60A Quick Fix

Intelligence, surveillance, and reconnaissance often focus on the air above the enemy. UAVs are weapons of choice for such a mission. In addition, there is a helicopter named Quick Fix that plays a significant role in military intelligence.

Quick Fix is a helicopter that can fight electronic warfare (see chapter 6). Quick Fix helicopters are used to support ground forces. The electronic countermeasures system called the AN/ALQ-151 provides information on specific targets and communications jamming for the commander. Quick Fix is capable of locating the enemy and preventing him or her from using his or her communications equipment.

The Prophet

The AN/MLQ-40, or Prophet, is a ground-based mobile SIGINT system. SIGINT involves the detection of enemy signals, such as radio signals.

The Prophet can survey the battlefield and provide early warning of potential threats. It provides the commander with an enhanced ability to see the battlespace. It is especially

The Prophet consists of a vehicle, computer equipment, and a signal interceptor. The vehicle is an HMMWV, which stands for high mobility, multi-purpose wheeled vehicle, and is also known as a Humvee. The HMMWV can carry up to four military intelligence personnel. They are responsible for operating the computer equipment and processing the information received by the signal interceptor.

helpful in determining enemy location, strength, and capabilities. The Prophet also assists in jamming enemy communications systems.

A BETTER WAY TO COMMUNICATE

There is no doubt that there is a tremendous amount of change taking place within the military intelligence community. Gone

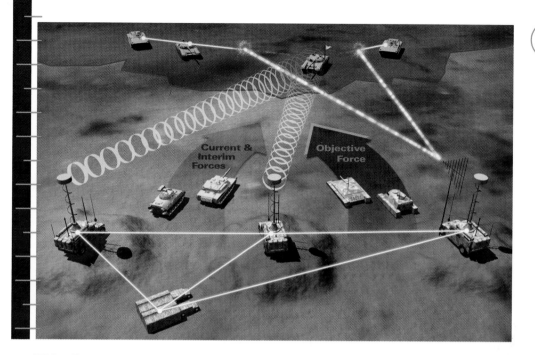

This diagram shows how the Prophet is used in warfare. The friendly force is depicted in the bottom half of the illustration, while the enemy force is above the jagged red line. During battle, the Prophet detects the presence of enemy vehicles. The location of the enemy vehicle is then passed on to tanks and other offensive weaponry. The Prophet can also jam enemy communications, making it difficult for the enemy to fight effectively.

are the days when researchers could develop a technology without considering how it fits in with other systems on the battlefield. The goal for the future in ISR is to create a system in which all the parts are interconnected. This system of systems will allow for seamless communication between all units in the military.

ANALYZING DATA TO SEE THE THREAT

The technologies discussed in the last two chapters are predominantly used to gather data. However, this data does not become useful to the military unless proper analysis is done. After analysis, the data becomes information. The military has identified future technologies that will help it effectively analyze collected data about the enemy and the battlespace and turn that data into useful information.

One of the most important qualities of these future technologies is that they will work quickly. The army's goal is to have all information reach the commander in near real time. This will provide the commander with a view of the battlespace that is as accurate as possible.

This chapter will look at the computer systems and other technologies that are being developed by the U.S. military to improve the conversion of data into information.

ALL SOURCE ANALYSIS SYSTEM

The All Source Analysis System (ASAS) is an army computer program that can analyze intelligence data from both military and civilian sources. It works with the Army Battle Command System and Force XXI Battle Command Brigade and Below system. These are systems that provide the commander with a complete understanding of what is going on in a portion of the battlespace.

ASAS is an automated information system that can be brought to the battlefield in a protected box. In short, it is designed to support intelligence and electronic warfare operations. It can also help identify enemy targets for the ground forces.

The duty of ASAS is to help information flow up and down the chain of military command. ASAS ties together the various sensors, processors, and communications systems used by the military. ASAS helps form a seamless intelligence system that supports commanders across the range of military operations.

The following are characteristics of ASAS:

- Consists of a lightweight computer with a core set of common applications. Depending on the mission, additional software is available. This may include software for sensor management or other types of ISR software.

- Is able to read data from a remote computer workstation.

- Gathers maps and other graphics concerning the battlespace from many different units.

A soldier uses the Force XXI Battle Command Brigade and Below system in this photograph. The system tracks friendly and enemy forces on a computer screen. Friendly forces are represented by blue icons, while the enemy is represented by red icons. The system is mounted inside a Humvee.

❭ Receives and processes reports and data received over the Global Information Grid to maintain awareness of the battlespace.

FORCE XXI BATTLE COMMAND BRIGADE AND BELOW

Force XXI Battle Command Brigade and Below (FBCB2) provides battle command information to combat leaders, frontline soldiers, and support troops. FBCB2 is compatible with the ABCS, allowing the two systems to communicate with each other and share important information.

FBCB2 can be used by all soldiers in all units. This system also allows brigade and battalion-level commanders to command when away from their operations centers. It also allows the commander to communicate with any other commander who is equipped with FBCB2.

GLOBAL COMMAND AND CONTROL SYSTEM

The Global Command and Control System (GCCS) is a vital communications system. It is designed to provide communications to a U.S. fighting force anywhere on the globe at any time. It is highly compatible with the other communications and computer systems used by different branches of the military. GCCS provides each soldier with the same real-time picture of the battlespace.

GCCS enables fusion, or the ability to gather data from many sensors, and creates a clear picture of the battlefield. The information portrayed includes the status and locations of friendly and hostile forces. It uses multimedia to help understand the battlefield. This understanding of the battlefield is known in the military as real-time shared situational awareness.

MEASUREMENT AND SIGNALS INTELLIGENCE

Measurement and signals intelligence (MASINT) uses sensors to learn about the enemy. Types of MASINT sensors include radar, laser, optical, heat, sound, and nuclear. The MASINT Processing and Analysis System (MPAS) will enable MASINT analysts to identify and access data from various sensors. For

The marines have developed a vehicle that can detect chemicals in a sample of soil. Pictured here are the two arms that the vehicle uses to gather samples. When the arms are lowered to the ground, soil attaches to the sticky wheels at the end of each arm. The soil is then analyzed to see if it contains any dangerous chemicals.

example, imagine the army trying to find an enemy truck that is carrying chemicals. MASINT systems allow the analyst to use a variety of sensors on aircraft and satellites, and even ground sensors that can gather samples of soil to identify enemy movements and what kind of cargo the enemy is carrying.

Today, MASINT technologies are rapidly improving. Data processing has become real time and is often incorporated within the sensor. In the past, this data was passed to an analyst to conduct the analysis. The new MASINT sensors allow the collection and analysis to take place all at once.

COUNTERINTELLIGENCE SYSTEMS

The Counterintelligence/Human Intelligence Information Management Systems (CHIMS) is a set of systems designed to provide computer-programming support for army counterintelligence and human intelligence (CI/HUMINT) information collection. The system helps interrogators and investigators organize information obtained from the enemy. This information is made available to the entire military intelligence community.

The Counterintelligence/Human Intelligence Automated Tool Set (CHATS) is a set of equipment used by human intelligence interrogators and investigators in the field. CHATS is composed of a laptop computer, a digital scanner that can scan confiscated documents, a digital camera to take pictures of detainees or anything else related to the mission, a color printer, a global positioning system receiver to help operators identify their location, an encrypted telephone that allows secret conversations, and various other useful items.

With CHATS, counterintelligence units may store collected information in a computer database. They are also able to connect information with digital photographs obtained of the enemy and other characteristics like vehicles and homes that are associated with an enemy force. Once this data is collected, CHATS enables the flow of information over a number of existing military and civilian communications. Therefore, information gained on a specific enemy can be transmitted to many other places using this technology.

While CHATS represents the hardware associated with this technology, the CI/HUMINT All Source Integration System (CHASIS) is a collection of software programs designed to operate on the CHATS hardware. The software includes a typical operating system (like Windows is for most home computer systems) and other common automation functions such as word processing and database management. This software allows the user to work at the secret and top-secret levels.

With CHASIS, counterintelligence units will be able to look for stored information in local databases and share databases with other units. Using this software, intelligence operators will also be able to interactively chat online and e-mail one another so that the information can be shared among all operators in the field.

COUNTERING TERRORISM WITH TECHNOLOGY

Changes in military intelligence technology are based upon the ongoing war against terrorism. The question we have to ask at this point is what technologies are necessary to defeat terrorism?

The first place we should explore for the future is information technology (IT). Information technology is essential to virtually all of the United States' critical infrastructures, from the air traffic control system to the aircraft themselves, from the electric power grid to the financial and banking systems, and from the Internet to communications systems. In sum, the reliance of all of the United States' critical infrastructures on IT makes any of them vulnerable to a terrorist attack.

Because the possible attacks on the U.S. IT infrastructure vary so widely, it is difficult to argue that any one type is

Computer technology is an important part of the current war against terrorism. In this photo, soldiers use computer software to create profiles of prisoners captured during the wars in Afghanistan and Iraq. The profiles of the prisoners include fingerprints, palm prints, and voice samples. This information allows the military to identify the prisoners if they are involved in any crimes, such as terrorist acts, in the future.

more likely than others. This is why it is important to make a long-term commitment to research and development that will strengthen the nation's computer and telecommunications networks. Such a program could improve the nation's ability to prevent, detect, respond to, and recover from terrorist attacks.

INFORMATION AND NETWORK SECURITY

Research in information and network security is relevant to the nation's counterterrorism efforts for several reasons. Everything from banking to military operations is being done over a computer network. There are many who hack into these systems to disrupt their normal use. This is called cybercrime (acts committed using a computer and the Internet to steal a person's identity, sell stolen goods, stalk victims, or disrupt operations with computer programming). The increase of cyber-crime suggests a corresponding increase in the likelihood of severe damage through cyberattacks, or an assault against a computer system or network to render it ineffective.

These IT attacks, if conducted at the same time as a physical attack such as a bombing on a building or facility of importance, can be especially disastrous. If the attacker can destroy a gov-ernment building, for example, and at the same time disrupt the communications network by hacking into a computer, the entire community may be affected. Additionally, if an attack like this takes place, it will be difficult for emergency services to respond given the lack of communications capability. This will result in an even greater loss of life and property.

Given the potential for attacks against IT, much research in information and network security has been done in the past and will continue in the future. This research can be grouped into five areas: authentication, detection, containment, recov-ery, and buggy code.

) Authentication is a process used to prove that people are who they say they are when they try to access a network. The most common form of authentication is a log-on password. A good authentication process prevents unauthorized parties from gaining access to a computer system to cause harm.

➤ Detection is the process of identifying intruders who are intending to commit cyberattacks. Much has been done with research and technology to identify when someone who shouldn't be there has found his or her way onto a network. However, because potential terrorists are cautious and attempt to hide their entry and mask their actions, developing technology to detect these invaders is a very challenging problem.

➤ Containment is necessary when an intruder finds his or her way successfully into a computer network and he or she has the ability to disrupt many activities. It is important to contain a hacker once he or she has been detected. Containment technology needs to be refined in the future so that when an attack takes place all can be done to limit the damage done by the hacker.

➤ Recovery includes backup and decontamination. It is the process of backing up the information that may be infected by a hacker so that if it is lost it can be recovered to its original state. This technology is usually found in the form of a backup disk drive. Decontamination is the process of "cleaning" the virus or whatever means the hacker uses to infect the computer or network. It also identifies those areas not affected by the attack.

➤ Buggy code results in a flawed computer program. It is much like having a computer virus. An approach to this problem is to ensure fixes are available and installed, even though the fixes themselves may carry risks such as exposing other software flaws.

COMMUNICATIONS, COMMAND, CONTROL, AND INTELLIGENCE FOR EMERGENCY RESPONSE

Communications, command, control, and intelligence (C3I) systems are critical to emergency responders such as police, firefighters, and emergency medical personnel. Emergency response to terrorist attacks includes a number of responding agencies and therefore can be a complex and difficult effort to organize. Future technologies will make it easier for everyone involved in the emergency response to better communicate and work together.

A panel of terrorism experts known as the Committee on the Role of Information Technology in Responding to Terrorism came up with the following list of challenges of developing technologies for C3I systems for emergency responders. The list is from a book published in 2003 entitled *Information Technology for Counterterrorism*.

- Different emergency responders must be able to communicate with each other and other agencies. Poor communications among responding agencies has been a challenge for many years. Therefore, there is a need for technology that will allow the different agencies to better communicate.

- Emergency situations result in increased demand on communications systems. Research needs to be done to develop technology to handle increased capacity during surge periods.

An operator points at one of the screens of a homeland security alert system. The system, known as Area Security Operations Command and Control (ASOCC), is just one of the many ways in which the U.S. government is using technology to fight terrorism. The ASOCC uses specially designed computer software to help connect more than forty homeland security agencies across the country.

❱ In responding to disasters, emergency-response managers need decision-support tools that can assist them in sorting, evaluating, filtering, and integrating information from a large volume of traffic.

❱ Database development and information-sharing tools need to be developed so that responders can gain information as to where people should go during an emergency (e.g., for evacuation purposes).

❱ Systems have to be developed to deploy sensors during an emergency to track the spread of nuclear or biological contaminants and to locate survivors.

) Locating people is a major problem when there is physical damage to a structure or an area. Therefore, technology must be developed to provide a universal picture of the area in which the terrorist attack or disaster occurred.

THE FUTURE OF COUNTERTERRORISM

Beyond C3I systems, there are a number of technologies being developed to combat terrorism in the future. Many of these technologies are already in use. They will continue to be improved upon, redesigned, and upgraded as scientists and technicians learn more about the technologies and the methods of the terrorists they are hoping to counter.

Data Mining

Data mining is a technique used to find patterns in large amounts of data. Military intelligence analysts use it to learn about the behavior of the enemy. For example, an analyst might look at the movements of an enemy unit over the last few months. The analyst might discover that the enemy unit tends to move at night shortly before it attacks. This information could be used to counter the moves of the enemy.

Robots

Robots are used in situations that are too dangerous for human soldiers. They combine state-of-the-art engineering and computer technology.

Robots are expected to be used more often in future warfare.
Pictured above is a robot known as the Talon. It is being operated by
the soldier on the far left. The Talon can carry as many as seven
cameras and can be armed with a weapon, such as an M-16 rifle.

Sensors

Sensors can be used to detect danger in the environment. For
example, a sensor might be used to detect the presence of toxic
chemicals in a water supply or the presence of deadly virus
particles inside an office building.

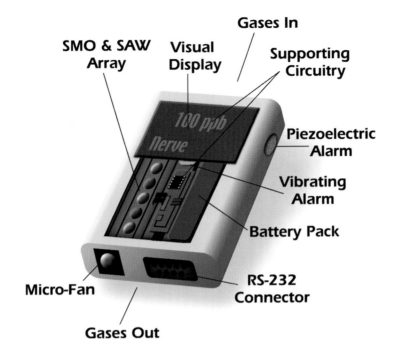

Gases In

SMO & SAW Array Visual Display Supporting Circuitry

100 ppb
Nerve

Piezoelectric Alarm

Vibrating Alarm

Battery Pack

Micro-Fan

RS-232 Connector

Gases Out

This is an illustration of a device that will be used by soldiers to detect dangerous chemicals in the air. It consists of multiple sensors that are programmed to detect chemical agents such as sarin and mustard gas. The device will be about the size of a wallet.

Modeling and Simulation

This technology consists of computer war games to simulate what might happen in the future. For years, the military has used this technology. In fact, in the months preceding Operations Desert Shield and Desert Storm in the Persian Gulf (1991), the U.S. military conducted a large-scale computer war game called *Intrinsic Action*. This game helped the military to come up with a strategy in case Iraq attacked south into Saudi Arabia. The lessons learned during that simulation were used to organize the deployment of forces to Saudi Arabia during the war.

ELECTRONIC WARFARE TECHNOLOGY

Electronic warfare has been around since the beginning of the twentieth century. It was used extensively during World War II (1939–1945), when both sides in the conflict used radar technology in order to gain an edge over the opponent. Electronic warfare has become more sophisticated in the years since World War II and will continue to grow more complex in the future.

Electronic warfare today includes the following technologies.

Electronic Countermeasures

This is the use of the electromagnetic spectrum (such as visible light, ultraviolet light, radio waves, microwaves, gamma rays, and X-rays) to deny use of the electromagnetic spectrum by the enemy. Most electronic countermeasures activity is in the form of jamming, which is used to limit the effectiveness of an opponent's communications equipment.

Much research has taken place to develop systems that will deny the enemy the use of the electromagnetic spectrum. The Tactical Jammer (TACJAM) technology is one of those systems that has existed for some years and is being refined to increase its capabilities. TACJAM technology is designed to deny, disrupt, or degrade enemy communications.

Another technology that is used for jamming, either from ground-mounted vehicles or on fast-moving aircraft, is called the AN/ALQ-99 Tactical Jamming System. It intercepts and processes radar signals to effectively jam large numbers of radar threats. As a result, enemy radar can't identify a U.S. aircraft and is unable to lock its missiles on the target and shoot the aircraft down.

A marine installs an electronic countermeasures device on an AH-1W Super Cobra helicopter. The device helps make the helicopter invisible to enemy radar and other communications systems. Radar is an electronic instrument that uses electromagnetic energy (radio waves) to detect distant objects.

Electronic Protective Measures

This technology ensures effective use of the electromagnetic spectrum in warfare despite the enemy's use of electronic warfare. Electronic protective measures include technical modifications to radio equipment so that it works regardless of the activity the enemy is taking to try to jam the radio.

Electronic Warfare Support Measures

This division of electronic warfare involves locating sources of electromagnetic energy in order to help identify the enemy. The Trailblazer AN/TSQ-138 is a system used for electronic warfare support. It is mounted on a tracked vehicle. The system is used to search for, intercept, record, identify, and report enemy radio signals. It can also operate with aerial systems such as the EH-60A Quick Fix. It will be set up in a unit's battlespace. Its antennae will detect enemy frequencies in use and then provide a direction and distance to the enemy location.

INFORMATION DOMINANCE

One of the purposes of electronic warfare is to gain information dominance against a foe. Information, and its control, is essential to success in future military operations. Access to information has been enhanced by the amazing automation available not only to the U.S. armed forces today but to potential enemies as well.

U.S. soldiers scale a wall during a nighttime raid in Tikrit, Iraq, on September 15, 2003. The raid was a result of information gathered by military intelligence soldiers. They had pinpointed the location of enemy combatants suspected of supporting the Iraqi dictator, Saddam Hussein. The raid resulted in the capture of five men and the discovery of a large store of weapons and cash.

Information dominance is a condition in which one army knows more about the battlespace than its enemy does. It is not a permanent condition and can be easily lost. Therefore, to be successful, the military must gather the information it requires and deny the enemy the information it needs. The military must be able to integrate information that it has acquired to put it to the best use. The linkage of information across many locations will produce a clearer picture of the battlefield. This will result in more science and less art put into decision making. In the end, technology can help achieve this desired goal.

SEEING THE FUTURE

The future of military intelligence technologies will focus on a better understanding of the battlespace. This will be accomplished through improved management of resources and seamless information sharing. As databases become more complex, the intelligence analyst has to use a wide variety of analytical skills supported by modern technology to better "see the enemy."

With the support of an advanced command, control, communications, computers, intelligence, surveillance, and reconnaissance (C4ISR) common backbone, the military of the future will be able to respond rapidly to any conflict. Through technology, warfighters will be better able to dominate any situation.

GLOSSARY

brigade Military unit consisting of 2,000 to 5,000 soldiers.

collateral damage Unintentional civilian casualties or destruction of civilian property during warfare.

counterintelligence The act of countering the intelligence gathering of spies or other enemies.

database An organized collection of data or information stored on a computer.

deploy To put into use.

division Military unit under the command of a major general consisting of about 15,000 soldiers.

electronic warfare A type of warfare in which the combatants fight to dominate the electronic flow of information.

information technology The hardware and software that is used to create, store, process, and transmit information electronically.

infrared Light waves that are just outside the red part of the visible spectrum.

infrastructure The basic facilities and services needed for a community to function.

interrogate A technique used to interview a person in order to get information about a crime or a military operation.

multimedia The combination of different media, such as audio, video, text, and graphics.

optical Pertaining to or using light.

platoon Military unit consisting of about forty soldiers.

sensor An instrument that reacts to a stimulus, such as heat, light, or sound, by generating a signal that can be measured.

telecommunications Electronic transmission of data, images, voice, or video over long distances.

terrain The surface features of a section of land.

tracked vehicle A type of vehicle that runs on tracks instead of wheels. A tank is an example of a tracked vehicle.

FOR MORE INFORMATION

Air Intelligence Agency
102 Hall Boulevard, Suite 234
San Antonio, TX 78243-7036
(210) 977-2166
Web site: http://aia.lackland.af.mil/aia

National Geospatial-Intelligence Agency
Public Affairs Division, MS D-45
4600 Sangamore Road
Bethesda, MD 20816-5003
(800) 455-0899
Web site: http://www.nima.mil

National Reconnaissance Office
14675 Lee Road
Chantilly, VA 20151-1715
(703) 808-1198
Web site: http://www.nro.gov

Office of Naval Intelligence
4251 Suitland Road
Washington, DC 20395-5720
(301) 669-5557
Web site: http://www.nmic.navy.mil

U.S. Army Intelligence Center
1903 Hatfield Street
Fort Huachuca, AZ 85613
(520) 533-3010
Web site: http://huachuca-www.army.mil

Web Sites

Due to the changing nature of Internet links, the Rosen Publishing Group, Inc., has developed an online list of Web sites related to the subject of this book. This site is updated regularly. Please use this link to access the list:

http://www.rosenlinks.com/lfw/mitf

FOR FURTHER READING

Burnett, Betty, Ph.D. *Delta Force: Counterterrorism Unit of the U.S. Army*. New York, NY: Rosen Publishing Group, 2003.

Evans, Nicholas D. *Military Gadgets: How Advanced Technology Is Transforming Today's Battlefield . . . and Tomorrow's*. Upper Saddle River, NJ: Prentice Hall, 2003.

Kupperberg, Paul. *Spy Satellites*. New York, NY: Rosen Publishing Group, 2003.

Poolos, J. *Army Rangers: Surveillance and Reconnaissance for the U.S. Army*. New York, NY: Rosen Publishing Group, 2003.

Vizard, Frank, and Phil Scott. *21st Century Soldier: The Weaponry, Gear, and Technology of the Military in the New Century*. New York, NY: Popular Science, 2002.

Yenne, Bill. *Attack of the Drones: A History of Unmanned Aerial Combat*. St. Paul, MN: MBI Publishing, 2004.

BIBLIOGRAPHY

Behling, Thomas, and Kenneth McGruther. "Planning Satellite Reconnaissance to Support Military Operations." Retrieved June 2, 2005 (http://www.milnet.com/cia/sat-recon/art10.html).

Dunbar, Richard. "Getting Out Front with Army Intelligence Modeling and Simulation." Retrieved June 2, 2005 (http://www.sisostds.org/webletter/siso/iss_102/art_585.htm).

Federation of American Scientists. "Intelligence Programs and Systems." Retrieved June 20, 2005 (http://www.fas.org/irp/program/list.htm).

Garrett, Darryl. "A Commitment for the Future." *Military Geospatial Technology*. September 28, 2004. Retrieved June 20, 2005 (http://www.military-geospatial-technology.com/article.cfm?DocID=632).

GlobalSecurity.org. "US Weapon Systems." Retrieved June 2, 2005 (http://www.globalsecurity.org/military/systems).

Global Transportation Network. "Source Systems Interfaces." Retrieved June 20, 2005 (http://gtnpmo.transcom.mil/information/gtninfo_source_sys_interfaces.html).

Hennessy, John L., Herbert Lin, and David A. Patterson, eds. *Information Technology for Counterterrorism: Immediate Actions and Future Possibilities*. Washington, DC: National Research

Council, 2003. Retrieved June 2, 2005 (http://www7.
nationalacademies.org/cstb/pub_counterterrorism.html).

Ingalls, W. Wayne. "Fires TTP to Defeat the COE OPFOR—
Contemporary Operational Environment—Tactics, Techniques and
Procedures." *FA Journal.* January–February 2003. Retrieved June 2,
2005 (http://www.findarticles.com/p/articles/mi_m0IAU/is_1_8/
ai_98123576).

Iwicki, Stephen K. "Synchronized Chaos: Visualization, Integration,
and Dynamic Thinking." *Military Intelligence Professional
Bulletin.* January–March 2003. Retrieved June 20, 2005 (http://
www.findarticles.com/p/articles/mi_m0IBS/is_1_29/ai_97822082).

Powell, Michael W. "MI Systems Transformation—United States
Army Planning Intelligence Systems Overhaul." *Military
Intelligence Professional Bulletin.* October–December 2000.
Retrieved June 2, 2005 (http://www.findarticles.com/p/articles/
mi_m0IBS/is_4_26/ai_78413211).

Thomas, Charles W., Major General, with Captain Cary C. Harbaugh.
"The Military Intelligence Vision for the XXI Century." *Military
Intelligence Professional Bulletin.* April–June 1996. Retrieved June
2, 2005 (http://www.fas.org/irp/agency/army/mipb/1996-2/
thomas.htm).

Titan National Security Solutions. "AN/MLQ-40(V)3 Multi-Sensor
SIGINT System—Prophet." Retrieved June 20, 2005 (http://www.
titan.com/products-services/load_pdf.html?filename=382__
1078019002.pdf).

United States Army. "Warfighter Guide to Intelligence 2000." August
1999. Retrieved June 2, 2005 (http://www.fas.org/irp/doddir/
army/wg2000/index.html).

INDEX

About the Author

Colonel Dominic J. Caraccilo is currently the operations officer for the 101st Airborne Division (Air Assault) deployed to Tikrit, Iraq, for Operation Iraqi Freedom. He holds a bachelor of science from the U.S. Military Academy at West Point, a master of science in operations research and industrial engineering from Cornell University, and a master of art in national security and strategic studies from the Naval War College. Caraccilo has served in Desert Shield/Desert Storm in command of a company with the 82nd Airborne Division, in Afghanistan as a member of the U.S. Army's 75th Ranger Regiment, and in Kirkuk, Iraq, as a battalion commander in the 173rd Airborne Brigade. He has also served as an assistant professor at the U.S. Military Academy at West Point.

Photo Credits

Cover U.S. Department of Defense courtesy photo; cover left corner © Digital Vision/Getty Images; top middle © Photodisc Red/Getty Images; p. 6 and throughout U.S. Navy photo by Photographer's Mate 1st Class Duckworth; p. 7 Cpl. Randy Bernard/U.S. Marines; p. 9 photo courtesy of U.S. Army/Fred W. Baker III; p. 11 © Lynsey Addario/Corbis; p. 13 Sgt. Donald Bohanner/U.S. Marines; p. 15 U.S. Army/FCS; pp. 17, 51 Cpl. Rocco DeFilippis; p. 19 DoD photo by Petty Officer 1st Class Jeremy L. Wood, U.S. Navy; p. 23 Official USMC photo; p. 27 © Getty Images; pp. 30, 32, 33 © 2005 General Dynamics C4 Systems; 36 Linda D. Kozaryn/Department of Defense; p. 38 Capt. Will Klumpp/U.S. Marines; p. 42 © John Miller/AP/Wide World Photos; p. 46 © Bill Haber/AP/Wide World Photos; p. 48 photo courtesy of U.S. Army/Sgt. Lorie Jewell; p. 49 Office of Naval Research; p. 53 © Rob Griffith/AP/Wide World Photos;

Designer: Evelyn Horovicz; Editor: Brian Belval